THE DOMINIE WO

What Is a Bird?

GRAHAM MEADOWS & CLAIRE VIAL

Contents

DOMINIE PRESS
Pearson Learning Group

About Birds

Birds are the only animals on Earth that have feathers. They are warm-blooded. They have two wings and a beak, which is also called a bill, and they lay eggs.

Most birds can fly. Birds that fly have hollow bones to help make their bodies weigh less. Birds that cannot fly, such as ostriches, have heavier, more solid bones.

A person who studies birds is called an ornithologist.

Australasian gannet

Ostrich

2

Eurasian blackbird

Birds' Place in the World of Animals

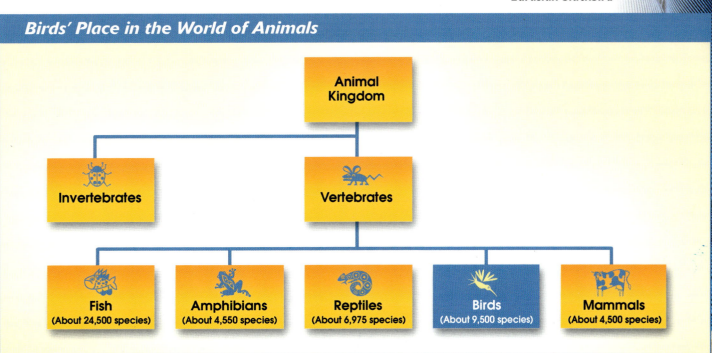

Animal Kingdom

- Invertebrates
- Vertebrates
  - Fish (About 24,500 species)
  - Amphibians (About 4,550 species)
  - Reptiles (About 6,975 species)
  - Birds (About 9,500 species)
  - Mammals (About 4,500 species)

3

How Birds Evolved

Scientists believe that birds **evolved** from ancient **reptiles** more than 200 million years ago, during the Triassic Period.

Like reptiles, the earliest birds had **scales** on their skin. These scales gradually evolved into feathers. The birds that we see around us today still have some scales, which are on their legs.

Dinosaurs ruled the world until they became **extinct** about 65 million years ago. At that time, **mammals** were still very small and could not compete with birds, which took over.

Song thrush

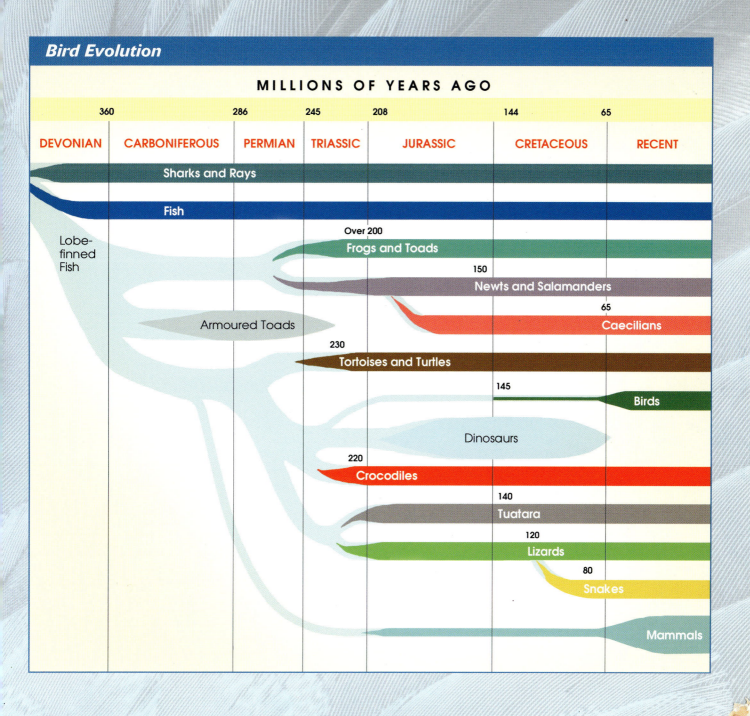

Bird Evolution

MILLIONS OF YEARS AGO

360	286	245	208	144	65
DEVONIAN	CARBONIFEROUS	PERMIAN	TRIASSIC	JURASSIC	CRETACEOUS	RECENT

Sharks and Rays

Fish

Lobe-finned Fish

Over 200
Frogs and Toads

150
Newts and Salamanders

65
Caecilians

Armoured Toads

230
Tortoises and Turtles

145
Birds

Dinosaurs

220
Crocodiles

140
Tuatara

120
Lizards

80
Snakes

Mammals

5

208	144		65
Jurassic	**Cretaceous**		

	Archaeopteryx (About 150 mya)	**Confuciusornis** (144-120 mya)	**Iberomesornis** (About 100 mya)	**Hesperornis** (80-65 mya)
How big was it?	About two feet tall	About one foot tall	About six inches tall	Up to six feet long
Could it fly?	Probably not	Yes, but not a strong flier	Yes, a strong flier	No
Did the beak have teeth?	Yes	No	Yes	Yes
What did it eat?	Invertebrates and lizards	Uncertain	Invertebrates	Fish
Other information	Found in Germany. *Archaeopteryx* means "ancient wing." It had three claws on each wing and a long, bony tail.	Found in China. *Confuciusornis* means "sacred bird of Confucius." It had three claws on each wing. It may have been one of the first birds that could fly well.	Found in Spain. *Iberomesornis* means "Spanish Bird."	Found in North America. *Hesperornis* means "western bird." had webbed feet. It wa probably a good swimmer and diver.

Ago (mya)

Recent

Present

Ichthyornis (80-65 mya)	Gastornis (46-41 mya)	Phorusrhacos (About 27 mya)	Dromornis (8-6 mya)	Teratornis (1 mya)
Up to one foot tall	Nearly six feet tall	About eight feet tall	Nearly ten feet tall	More than ten feet long. Wingspan, twenty-five feet.
Yes, a strong flyer	No	No	No	Yes
Yes	No. Beak was huge and hooked.	No. Beak was huge and hooked.	No. Beak was large.	No
Fish	Various animals	Various animals	Plants and possibly meat	Various animals
Found in North America. *Ichthyornis* means "fish bird." It probably dived from the air to catch fish, much like gannets do today.	Found in Germany and the United States. Scientists think Gastornis could have hunted small horses.	Found in South America. Belonged to a group called the Terror Birds. They became extinct about 15,000 years ago.	Found in Australia. Belonged to a group called Thunderbirds. It was the biggest bird that ever lived, weighing more than 1,000 pounds.	Found in the La Brea tar pits, California, and Argentina. *Teratornis* means "monster bird." It was like a large condor. Possibly the largest flying bird of all time, weighing about 250 pounds.

The little blue penguin of Australasia is the smallest penguin.

The brown kiwi of New Zealand is nocturnal.

Types of Birds

Today there are about 9,500 bird **species**, which vary in shape, size, and color. Scientists classify them into about twenty-seven groups, called orders. The birds in each order are closely related to each other and have many features in common.

Some birds, such as ostriches and kiwis, are flightless. Others, such as penguins, spend much of their lives in water.

The golden-breasted starling of Africa is a perching, or passerine, bird.

| **Birds** |
| About 27 orders: 9,500 species |

| **Perching Birds** (Passerine Birds) | **Non-Perching Birds** (Non-Passerine Birds) |
| One order with about 5,300 species | About 26 orders with about 4,200 species |

The greater African flamingo is a non-perching, or non-passerine, bird.

9

The chestnut-bellied sandgrouse lives in dry habitats.

Where Birds Are Found

Birds are found on all **continents**, and on almost every island, in the world. Some species, such as the house sparrow, are found in many different countries.

Other species are found in only one country. For example, the takahe, which is an **endangered** bird, lives only in New Zealand.

Birds can be found in many different **habitats**. About two-thirds of all birds live in **tropical** rain forests.

Some species, such as snowy owls, are found only in the **Northern Hemisphere**. Other species, such as penguins, are found only in the **Southern Hemisphere**.

Takahe

Male house sparrow

Mallards live in wet habitats.

Emu

Mute swan

Their Bones

Birds that fly have a lightweight skeleton. Many of their bones are hollow and look like a honeycomb inside.

In many flightless birds, such as the emu, the bones are solid.

All mammals have seven neck bones, called vertebrae. Birds have more than seven vertebrae. For example, a mute swan has twenty-five.

In many flying birds, the breastbone is very large. It has a **keel** where the flight muscles attach. Most flightless birds have a small keel on their breastbone.

The collarbone, or wishbone, acts as an extra support when birds are flying. The tailbones are very small.

Domestic Pigeon Skeleton

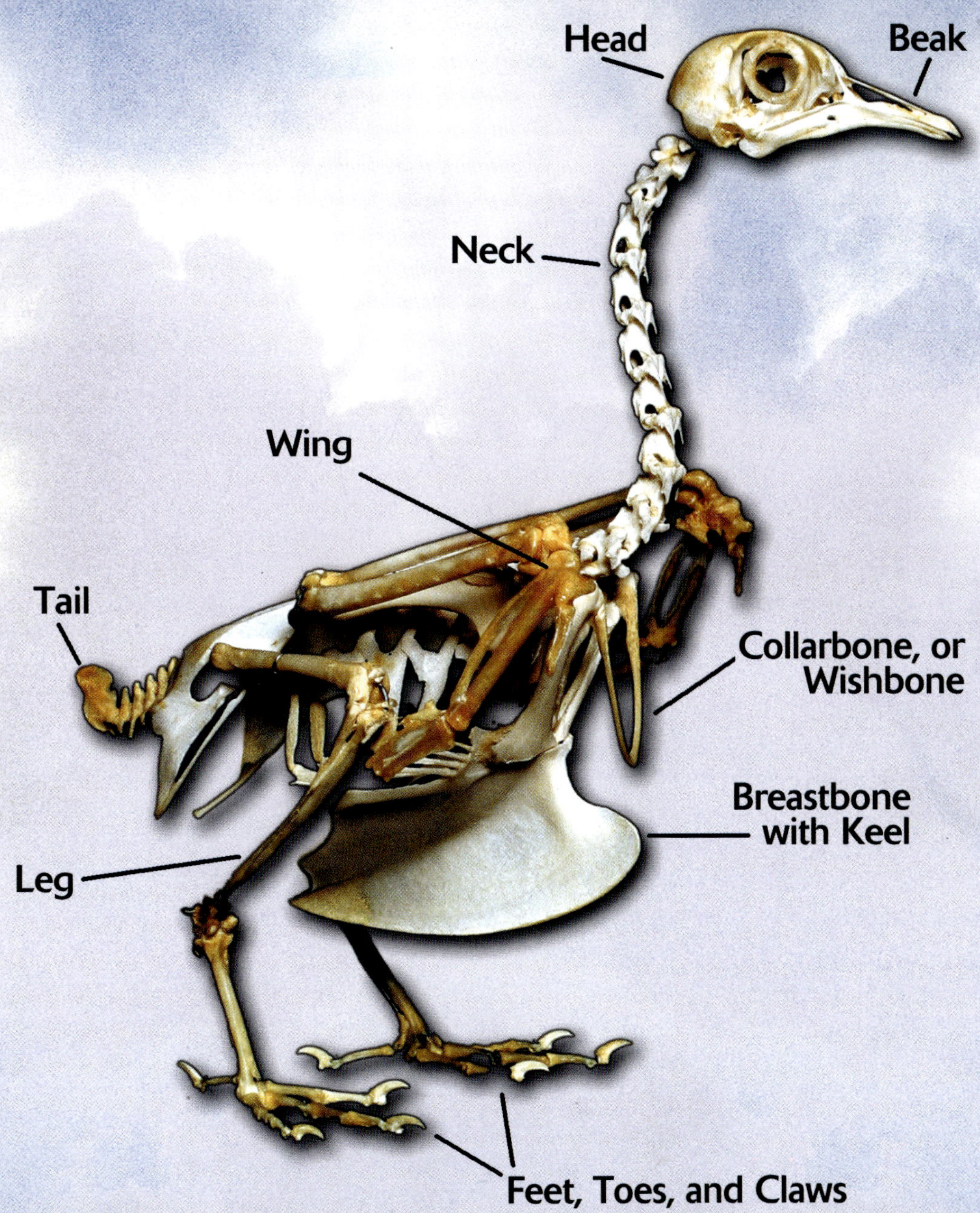

Head

Beak

Neck

Wing

Tail

Collarbone, or Wishbone

Breastbone with Keel

Leg

Feet, Toes, and Claws

The rainbow lorikeet is very colorful.

This gray duck is preening.

Their Feathers

Feathers are made up of keratin, the same substance our fingernails are made of.

Feathers come in many different colors, including brown and black.

Birds have several different types of feathers, including flight feathers for flying, tail feathers for steering, and down feathers for warmth. They also use their feathers for display, **camouflage**, and protection.

Many birds have a special oil gland at the base of their tail. They spread this oil on their feathers when they are preening, or **grooming** themselves. This keeps the feathers waterproof.

Because feathers wear out, most birds replace, or regrow, them once a year. This replacement process is called **molting**.

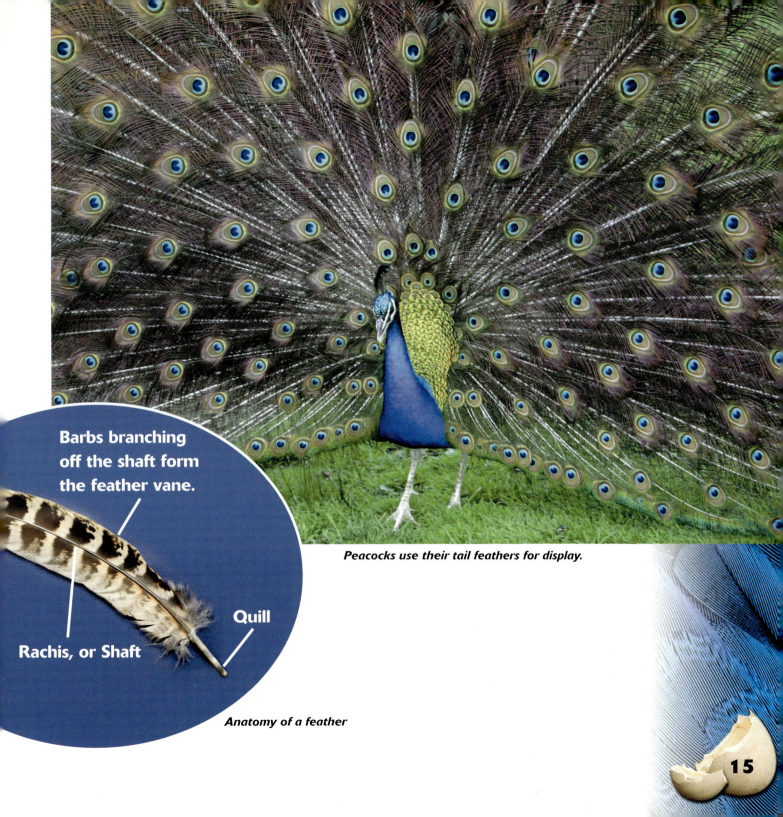

Barbs branching off the shaft form the feather vane.

Quill

Rachis, or Shaft

Anatomy of a feather

Peacocks use their tail feathers for display.

Their Beaks and Nostrils

Birds have lightweight beaks made of keratin. The shape of the beaks differs from one species to another. Most birds use their beaks to catch and carry their food.

Parrots, such as macaws, have strong, hooked beaks to crack and eat nuts and seeds.

Kiwis have long, thin beaks to probe the soil for **invertebrates**.

Flamingos have a curved beak with bristles to filter tiny animals and plants from the water.

Finches have a short, strong, stubby beak to crack and eat seeds.

Wading birds, such as the godwit, have a long, thin beak to probe sand and mud for invertebrates.

Birds of **prey**, such as eagles, have a strong, hooked beak to hold, kill, and eat other animals.

Blue-and-yellow macaw

Brolga crane

Brown kiwi

Cranes have a long, sharp, pointed beak to catch and eat small animals.

Birds have nostrils on their beaks. They use their nostrils for breathing and smelling. The position of the nostrils varies among species. Most birds have a poor sense of smell. Instead, they rely on their senses of sight and hearing to **survive**.

Turkey vultures have a **keen** sense of smell. They can smell dead animals from a long distance.

Godwit

Greater African flamingo

Bald eagle

Zebra finch

17

Swinhoe's pheasant

Emu

 # Their Eyes and Ears

Sight is a bird's most important sense. A bird's eyes are large when compared to the size of its skull. Birds cannot swivel their eyeballs very far. Instead, they turn their heads.

Most birds have eyes on the sides of their head, and they can see almost all around them.

Owls have eyes on the front of their head. They look forward to focus on their prey, and they can judge distances accurately.

Hearing is a bird's second-most important sense. Unlike humans, a bird's ears do not stick out from its head. In most birds, the ears are covered by feathers. One exception is the emu.

Birds have a third eyelid, called a nictitating membrane, which moves across the eye to protect it.

Rameron pigeon

A Eurasian eagle owl has tufts of feathers on its head. These are not ears.

19

Ostriches have thick pads underneath their toes.

New Zealand scaup

Their Feet and Claws

The shape of birds' feet varies among species. Most birds have four toes. Emus and rheas have three toes, and ostriches have two.

Ducks, such as the New Zealand scaup, have webs between their toes to help them swim.

Birds of prey, such as hawks, use long, sharp claws, called talons, to catch and kill their prey.

Parrots, such as cockatoos, use their strong claws to hold on to branches and food. Two of their toes point forward, and two toes point backward.

Wading birds, such as the black-winged stilt, have long toes for walking on soft mud and sand.

Perching birds, such as the red bishop, have three toes pointing forward, and one toe pointing backward.

Pheasants and fowls, such as hens, have strong, hard claws for digging and scratching the ground.

Domestic hen

lack-winged stilt

ulphur-crested cockatoo

Hawk with prey

Red bishop

21

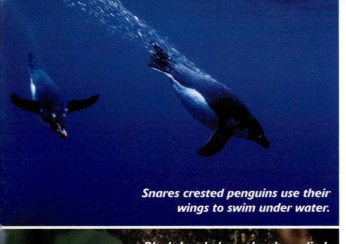

Snares crested penguins use their wings to swim under water.

Black-headed woodpeckers climb trees, searching for food.

How Birds Move Around

Different species of birds move around in different ways. Most birds can fly from place to place. Some birds hop, walk, or run along the ground. Others swim on or under water.

Great egrets fly between wetlands to feed.

Hummingbirds hover while feeding on nectar.

Ostriches can run up to thirty-five miles per hour.

Giant wood rails walk around wetlands, looking for food.

Black swans use their feet to swim along the surface of the water.

23

Glossary

camouflage: A blending into the immediate surroundings to avoid being seen by predators or prey

continents: The largest land masses on Earth; there are seven continents—Africa, Antarctica, Asia, Australia, Europe, North America, and South America

endangered: Threatened with extinction

evolved: Underwent gradual physical changes over time

extinct: Disappearance of a species

grooming: Cleaning behavior in animals and humans

habitats: The places where animals and plants live and grow

invertebrates: Animals that do not have a backbone

keel: A ridge-shaped part of an organism

keen: Sharp; very sensitive

mammals: A class of warm-blooded animals in which the female feeds her young with her own milk

molting: Periodically shedding feathers, hair, or skin and replacing what is lost with new growth

Northern Hemisphere: The half of Earth located north of the equator

prey (n): Animals that are hunted and eaten by other animals

reptiles: Cool-blooded vertebrates with dry, scaly skin, belonging to the class Reptilia

scales: Small, flattened plates that form the outer covering of an animal's body or a portion of its body

Southern Hemisphere: The half of Earth located south of the equator

species: A group of animals or plants that have many physical characteristics in common

survive: To stay alive and thrive

tropical: Describing areas of land or sea that are very warm throughout the year and lie between the tropic of Capricorn and the tropic of Cancer

Index